The Peninsula

Ramsthal's Nagawicka Lake Subdivision

A History

Nagawicka Lake Delafield, Wisconsin

The Cottage built by Theodore and Bertha Koepp Ramsthal

By James Halstead Smith

This book represents a collection of archived material, photographs from family members and copies of whole maps or portions of maps. Maps that are included have been purchased as copies of the originals by the author. Archived information from the Waukesha County, WI, Register of Deeds has been downloaded after purchasing the same online.

ISBN: 979-8-218-86294-7

Printed 2025

Printed in the United States of America

Unprovided with original learning, unformed in the habits of thinking, unskilled in the arts of composition, I resolved to write a book.

The quote above is from the English author, Edward Gibbon (1737-1794), who wrote <u>The History of the Decline and Fall of the Roman Empire</u>.

With the above disclosure, I decided to write this book about a small peninsula on the west side of Nagawicka Lake, Delafield, WI.

Acknowledgments

This book would not have been possible and written without the help of many people.

My aunt, Joan Brenkus Jensen, provided information that no one else would have known. The first was that bogs in the area would be used to further connect what was perhaps a sliver of ground to the mainland shore. She also was the source of many family photos…and the identities of the people when no names had been written on the back of the photos.

To my first cousin, Jenny Jensen (Joan's daughter), who also provided early photos taken at Nagawicka Lake and the dates of the photos. While going through old boxes of family history, she discovered some old family videos. She sent one of the videos to be professionally digitized into a format that can be read by today's computers. The author met with Joan and Jenny in June 2024 to review the video to determine who the people were and to calculate the year it was taken based on factors such as age for children. There are several still shots from this video that are included in this book. The first part of the video seems to be dated 1931. This is based on a young girl that seemed to be approximately 7 years old. The young girl, Patricia Jean McNamara Smith, is my mother. The video then seems to jump about three years to 1934 when two babies are included. Those two babies are my aunt Joan, born Sep 29, 1933 and her first cousin, William Kenneth Eichfeld, born Jan 31, 1934 and are shown as young infants.

To Hayes and Sandy Hatfield for photographs and their knowledge of Lot 6 on the peninsula. They provided invaluable assistance in reviewing/editing the material used in this book so that it reads more smoothly.

To the volunteer staff at the Hawks Inn and Delafield History Center with their knowledge of Nagawicka Lake and the City of Delafield. Their critical knowledge was very helpful in developing a chronology of events 100+ years ago.

To my friends, Martin and Ann Marie McNamara, Nashville, Tennessee who met at St. John's Summer Camp which is located adjacent to Nagawicka Lake.

Items of Note: All documents presented in this book have been paid for (from the Waukesha County Register of Deeds office) and downloaded for inclusion in this book. Some of these documents were not included in the book itself but do provide background or additional information to those that were included. All photographs in the book have been supplied from family members…which includes the granddaughter or eight great grandchildren of Theodore and Bertha Ramsthal. A few photographs were given to me by Hayes and Sandy Hatfield and a couple from a former owner of Lot 5.

Background

The purpose of this book is to provide and share some history about this little peninsula on Nagawicka Lake. My maternal grandmother's father, Theodore Frank Ramsthal, purchased this land which lies not quite half-way up the west side of the lake.

Theodore F. Ramsthal (1870-1943) and his wife, Bertha Koepp Ramsthal (1877-1937), the purchasers of the peninsula, had two daughters, Eleanor Bertha Minnie Ramsthal (1901-1991) and Leona Pauline Ramsthal (1903-1985). Eleanor had two daughters and I am one of eight grandchildren descended from Eleanor. Leona had one son and one grandson.

I was interested in when Theodore and Bertha purchased this piece of ground and how did they prepare it for sale to others to build a cottage? Who were the original lot owners and when did they buy their lots?

Officially, this peninsula is known as Ramsthal's Nagawicka Lake Subdivision on the records at Waukesha County Register of Deeds.

Nagawicka Lake lies within the U.S. Public Land Survey Sections 5, 8, 9, 16, 17, 20, and 21, Township 7 North, Range 18 East in north-central Waukesha County, Wisconsin. The Lake is located partially in the City of Delafield and partially in the Village of Nashotah, and is on the fringe of metropolitan Milwaukee. *Source: SEWRPC Community Assistance Planning Report No. 262, 2nd Edition. A LAKE MANAGEMENT PLAN FOR NAGAWICKA LAKE, WAUKESHA COUNTY, WISCONSIN. Chapter 1 INTRODUCTION*

The Ramsthals Nagawicka Lake Subdivision is located in the southwest corner of Section 8. Thus, the legal description taken from a Plat of Survey is:

Ramsthal's Nagawicka Lake Subdivision, being a part of the North 60 acres of the South ½ of the SW ¼ of Section 8, T (town) 7N, R (range). 18E., City of Delafield, Waukesha County, Wisconsin.

An internet search on the name, Nagawicka, revealed that it means "**there is sand**," and has a maximum depth of 90 feet. It gets its name from the numerous sand bars to the west of St. John's Island and along the western shoreline that make for excellent swimming spots. The photo below is an aerial photograph taken in 2022. It shows a lighter green color on the right hand side which appears to be the sandbar running north and south. The aqua(ish) highlighted area on the left is Lot 6 of the subdivision and was the lot that the Ramsthals put their cottage on.

The Players

The main players of this book can be found in this photograph: **Theodore F. Ramsthal** (1870-1943) is standing on the back row in the middle with his arms folded. Standing next to him (on the right) is his daughter **Leona Ramsthal** Eichfeld (1903-1985). On the middle row seated: the woman, second from the right in a dark dress, is **Bertha Koepp Ramsthal** (1877-1937), Theodore's wife. To the right of Bertha is **Eleanor Ramsthal** Brenkus (1901-1991). Eleanor was the eldest daughter of Theodore and Bertha and would marry twice: first to Leo P. McNamara and second to Louis F. Brenkus. While no date was written on the photo, I am estimating it to be 1928. I am using the young boy who is sitting on his mother's lap in the middle row to arrive at this date. His name is Richard Huebner and he was born in 1926. Richard was killed in action on Jan 7, 1945 during World War II at the Battle of the Bulge. I am estimating that Richard was two years old in this photo. That would make Theodore 58 years old in 1928. As will be shown later, he started selling lots on the peninsula the year before in 1927.

Theodore was a second generation American from Germany (he was the first generation to be born in America). He spent his entire working career in the mattress business. Federal Census data over three decades shows that he was variously listed as a mattress: maker/repairer, filler and/or upholsterer. Bertha was also a second generation American from Germany (first generation to be born in America). Her father was a shoemaker.

Chapter 1. In The Beginning

I am a big fan of maps, especially old maps. They provide a wealth of information based on the data that were available at the time of publication.

For comparative purposes only, I display below two old maps. The one on the left is dated 1851 and is an image from an internet search of old maps. This 1851 map shows the water level of the lake prior to the creation of the dam at the foot of the lake. Nelson P. Hawks built the Hawks Inn in Delafield as a stage coach stop in 1846. Research indicates that he built a dam in the 1850s to power a mill. Note the significant amounts of bog along the western shore of the lake.

The map on the right is dated 1891 and shows a significant increase in the size of the lake forty years later. The full-sized 1891 map that I purchased is presented on the following page with additional information.

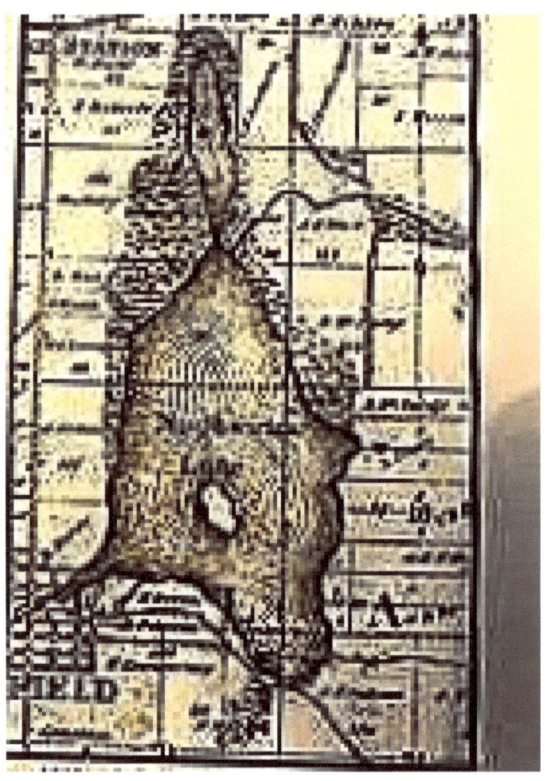

1851

1891

The purpose of the map comparison above is to show that a large portion of this boggy area was covered by the rising water level over a period of 40 years. That said, there were still some small areas of land along the west coastline that had some shallow water touching it.

I purchased a copy of this 1891 map from Interior Elements, Eagle WI (a shop that provides art publishing services to both retail and wholesale customers). The detail of the map, as far as the shoreline goes, is certainly not as detailed as newer maps. However, what intrigued me was the additional feature that showed the names of landowners surrounding Nagawicka as of 1891. One of my objectives was to determine which landowner(s) might have sold it to Theodore and Bertha.

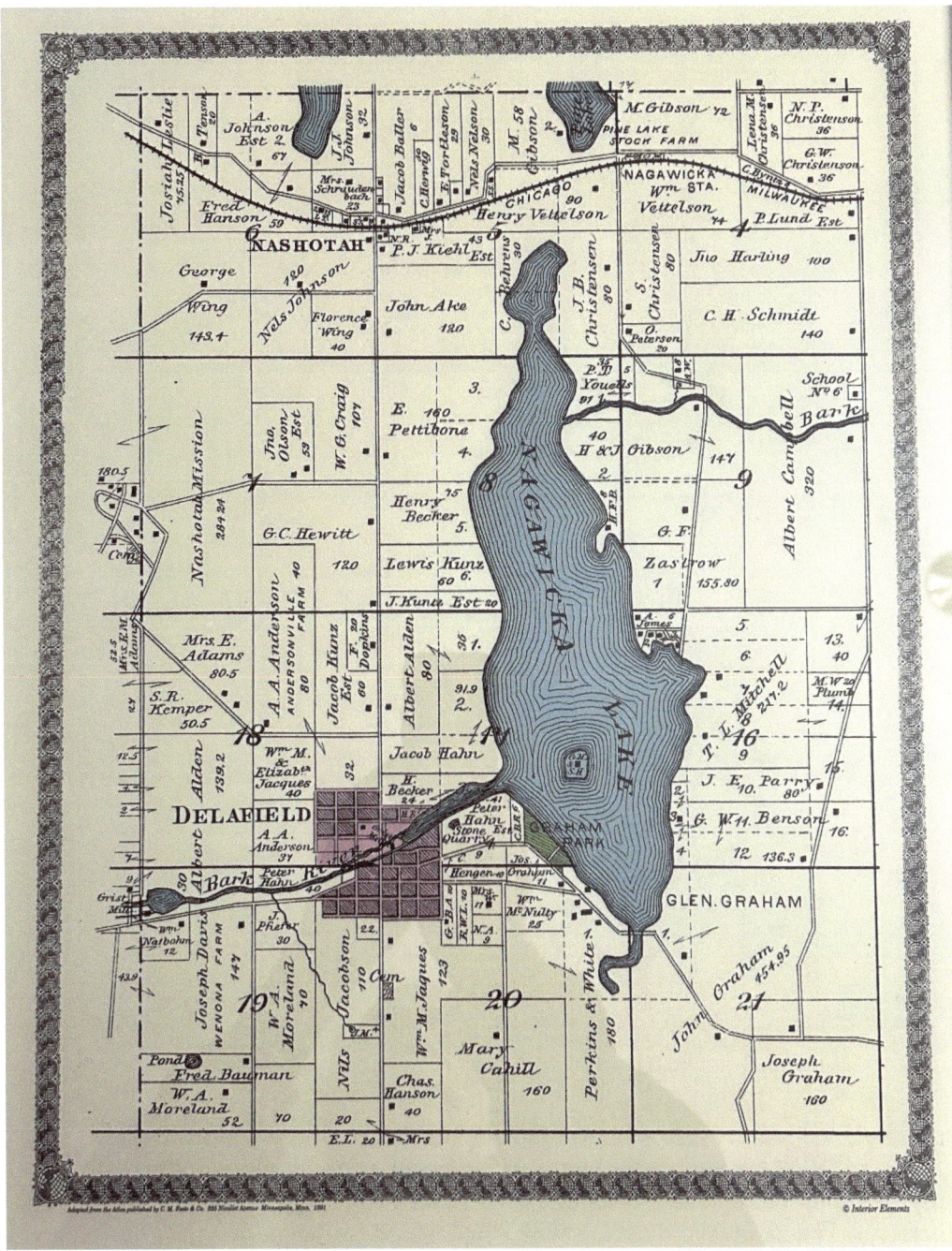

Also displayed here is a second map of Nagawicka Lake and Delafield, WI. It is also dated 1891 and provides a zoomed out view which includes the western portion of Pewaukee Lake.

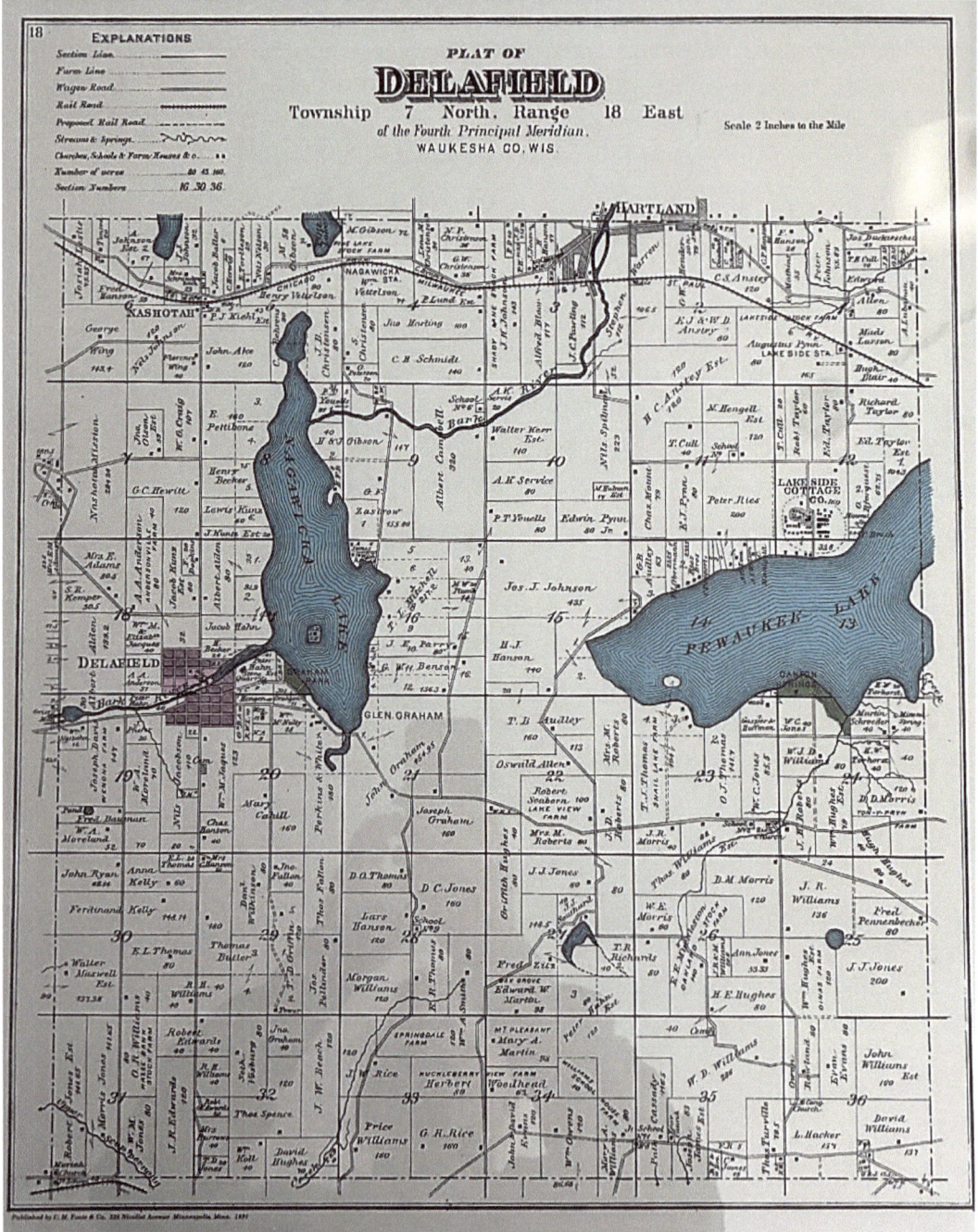

Courtesy of Interior Elements, Eagle, WI.

These maps helped provide confirming information on who owned various tracts of property in 1891, now known as the Ramsthals Nagawicka Lake Subdivision.

Family stories have been handed down from generation to generation to include that the peninsula had been an island (at the time of purchase by Theodore and Bertha) and that it (the island) had to be connected to the shore to become a peninsula. However, I could find no corroborating evidence to support that theory/story.

What I suspect is that the peninsula had become such once the water level increased sufficiently to be accessed on foot from the lake shoreline. How wide (from top to bottom) that section was at the bottom of the peninsula is probably lost to history. At the time of purchase, was access to the land walkable? Probably. Did Theordore need to fill in the land (at the bottom) to make it more accessible…either by walking or by driving over via an automobile or truck? Again, probably.

I think the best and most accurate answer is that Theodore filled in some amount of land by cutting into the bog from a scow (a flat bottomed boat). How much work he may have done is unknowable.

We are not absolutely certain when he did that work but that would have been sometime between the purchase date in 1912 and 1927 when he sold the first lot. However, we ARE certain that he used his scow to:
- Cut into the bog;
- Lift that piece of bog onto the scow;
- Let the bog completely dry;
- Then would push the dried bog onto the ground to fill in where he needed to.

The photo below is a still shot from a family video taken circa 1931 showing Theodore standing on his scow cleaning out the channel behind Lot 6.

We have copies of some Ramsthal family photos and I present the following photograph:

Written on the back of this photograph is: Lake Nagawicka Channel. It is undated. Since this photograph was from a family album, I am making the assumption that Theodore took it…or had someone take it. It is hard to determine the orientation of the photographer and whether he was standing on Theodore's island or on the mainland shore.

However, the more I looked at it, I formed the opinion that the photographer was standing on the peninsula. The trees in the foreground appear to be deciduous (versus evergreen). If so, the soil required to grow a deciduous tree would have to be more dense…regular dirt. It also appears that the land in the distance was bog. If my assumptions are correct, then this <u>general</u> area could have been where Theodore would have 'cut' the bog and drag that 'cut' onto his scow (flat bottomed boat) where it would then have dried out. The dried, cutout bog would have then been dropped back into the water at the shoreline to shore up the land to the Ramsthal peninsula.

Chapter 2. Early History of the Peninsula

The following photos also come from our family's photograph albums. They are dated but do not have any names associated with them. There was nothing written down verifying that these photos were taken on the peninsula. As will be shown later, Theodore and Bertha purchased this tract of land in 1912, so it would not be too big a stretch to think these might be the earliest photos of the peninsula.

The date of this first photo is 8/26 1914, but the location was not identified.

Perhaps it's wishful thinking, but after gathering all the information for this book, this MAY be the side view of the *original* cottage that sat on what would be Lot 6 of Ramsthal's Nagawicka Lake Subdivision. See also the photo below.

If one looks at the landscape on the far shore in the photo above, dated August 1916, this cottage could have been located on what is now Ramsthals Nagawicka Lake Subdivision. Notice the distant shore of the lake…it seems to be a very close resemblance to how it appears today in 2024. Could this second photo be the side yard to the first photo, dated Aug 26, 1914 on the previous page?

My cousin Jenny Jensen thinks the woman in the photo is Bertha Koepp Ramsthal. I tend to agree based on other photos we have of her. If our assumptions are correct, then who are the children? Bertha's daughters, Eleanor and Leona would have been 15 and 13, respectively in 1916. These children could possibly be a niece and nephews to Bertha. Theodore had 6 siblings and Bertha had 9 siblings so there would have been a large number of nieces and nephews from those siblings. It's at least conceivable.

If this cottage is, in fact, on Lot 6 of the Peninsula in 1916, it had to have been torn down at some point after that. The cottage that replaced it does not have the same front elevation nor the side elevation as this one.

The photo below, also dated August 26, 1914, and has South Park written on the back. Research, to date, has not revealed whether South Park was located at Nagawicka Lake or Delafield, WI.

Chapter 3. Lot Ownership

Prior to the sale of any of the five buildable lots, Theordore and Bertha needed to secure legal access to the peninsula. This was accomplished on Jun 12, 1925 as can be seen here in Vol 192, Page 43, Document # 138552. To get to the peninsula required traveling east along Woodland Park Road off Genesee Road. This road made a 90 degree turn to the north as it approached the channel/peninsula of what is now the Ramsthal's Nagawicka Lake Subdivision. A small portion (width of 30') of the west side of Lot 32 that was located in Barrack's Woodland Park subdivision was purchased from the owners, John and Clara Winkleman, of the corner lot on Woodland Park Road. The Ramsthals needed 30' of land on that particular tract so that they could connect with their peninsula along with the rights to use this section for ingress and egress. This new road would eventually be named Lakeview Court.

A couple of years after the purchase of the Barrack's Woodland Park tract, a walking bridge appears in the first photo on the following two pages. The back of the photo has **1927 ?** written on it. This date (1927) coincides with the first lot sales of the peninsula Lots that year. Based on this photo, it appears that there is still some water that had to be crossed to reach the peninsula.

Other verbiage on the back of the photo is interesting but I could not draw any definitive conclusions on exactly what had been done to the shoreline. One possible explanation on the wording on the back of the photo is that Al built the walking bridge. If the right hand side of the photo is the shoreline of the lake, then the amount of bog Theodore needed to fill in to connect to the island would suggest he still had a ways to go.

Again, armed with this photo and the date of **1927 (?)** , evidence suggests this bridge was completed that year, and prior to the sale of three lots later in 1927.

Author's side note (1): The questions/comments listed here do not have a clear answer. It appears that during 1927 that Theodore was preparing the south end of the peninsula and otherwise getting things lined up for the sale of the five lots. When and why did he choose to keep Lot 6 for himself and Bertha rather than Lot 7 which would otherwise be considered the best lot because it was at the end of the peninsula? The short answer is unknown. A longer answer was supplied by Joan Jensen in that she remembered Bertha had a burr under her saddle that Theodore did not keep Lot 7 for themselves.

Author's side note (2): The real answer is probably lost to history, but I proffer an opinion about the two photographs shown on pages 13 and 14. Evidence (that will be presented later) shows that Theodore and Bertha purchased the land in 1912. I think that there is a reasonable chance the peninsula was being used by the Ramsthals after that purchase. Is the cottage shown in those two photographs a predecessor to the cottage that was delivered sometime after the sale of Lot 5? (see pages 26 and 27)

AT THE "BRIDGE"

KAY AND ME

THE BRIDGE
IN
THE
CHANNEL
~~~

Nagawicka

The back of the photo is presented here.

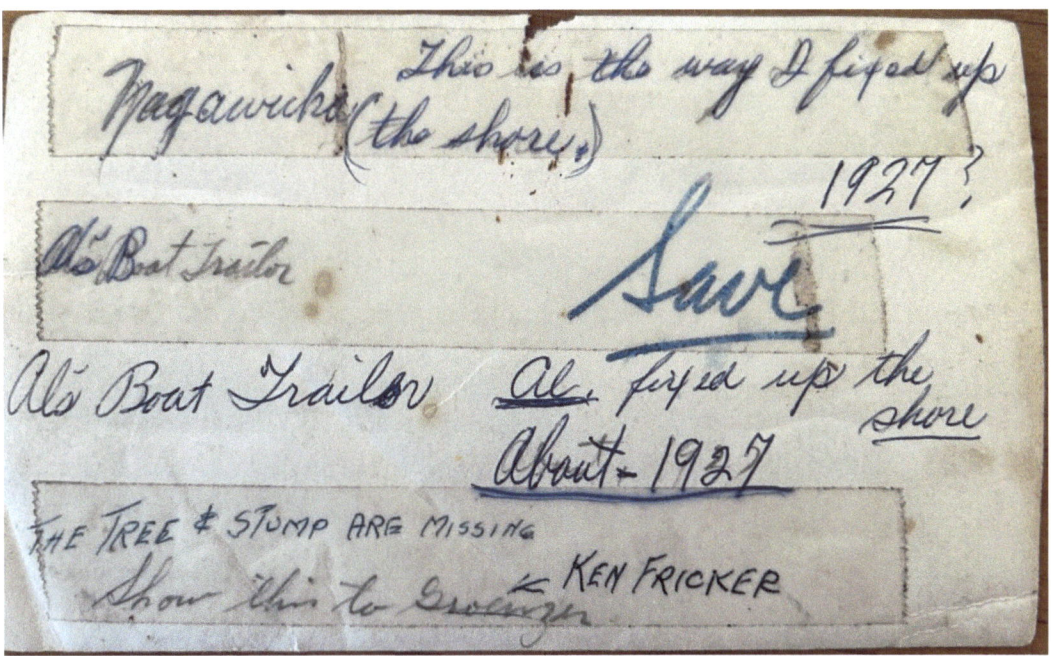

Let's only hope that Ken Fricker showed this photo to Groewzer (sp ?). And! Were the tree and stump ever found?! Inquiring minds want to know.

One of the earliest documents showing the various lots is from the Register of Deeds website is a survey of the peninsula and is shown below. It is Volume 9, Page 46, Document # 150626, and is dated Jun 3, 1927. This particular document appears to be the original survey of the entire peninsula property. It is a two page document with the first page being a sketch of the property...much like what one would find as part of a developer's architectural rendering. This first page provided a plethora of background information.

Some of the details are as follows:

The land (identified as 'Drive Way') was fully in place as of June 1927. The sketch's orientation shows that North is pointed to the top of the page.

There are architectural lines running roughly east to west which delineates the southern and northern property lines for the seven lots. Lot # 1 begins at the southern end and then proceeds to Lot # 7 at the tip of the peninsula.

The first page is the sketch of the Ramsthal's Nagawicka Lake Subdivision. The second page is some required survey verbiage but does not add any pertinent information and thus, is not included in this book. The sketch did provide some information that I was not expecting. This shows that 1927 was the beginning of the subdivision as it exists today.

Note: Online research through the Waukesha County Register of Deeds and the GIS department show that Theodore's original plan was to have 7 lots. Those seven lots are still designated on the books. Since Lot owners needed a place to park their cars, Lot 1 became designated as the parking area. Additionally, Lot 4 may have been too narrow to build a cottage on and it was split up into Lot 3 and Lot 5. Thus, there were only five buildable lots.

Apologies for the shading of this document.

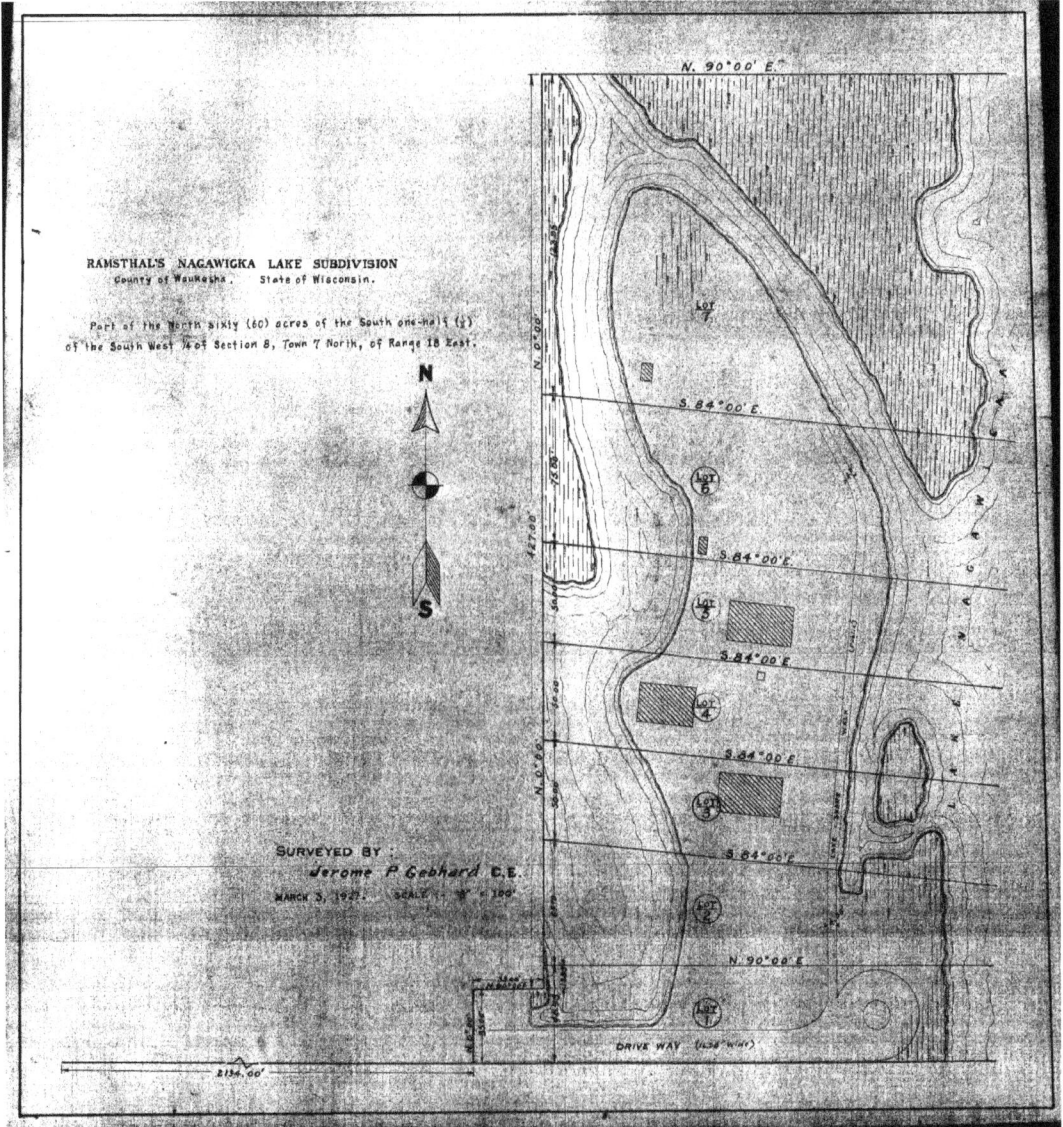

Some takeaways from this document which is dated Mar 3, 1927.

- There was a sizable amount of bog on the lakefront side of Lot 7 and half of Lot 6.
- There are three structures of some sort. Lots 3, 4 and 5.
- The structure on Lot 4 that may have been a shed rather than a cottage.
- There is a small bog island on the lakefront side of Lots 3 and 4.
- There is a large bog on the lakefront side of Lots 1 and 2 and part of 3.
- There is still some bog in the channel behind Lots 5, 6 and 7.

First Sale. Lot 2. The sale to Henry Schumann and his wife Molly Schumann on Jul 5, 1927, was the first of the five lots that were sold.

An Ancestry.com research revealed the following about the first owners. Henry Schumann was born in Wisconsin in 1865 and was the first generation in his family to be born in America. His wife, Molly (a/k/a Mollie), was born in Germany. According to the 1910 Federal Census, the Schumanns lived at 323 Harmon Street, Milwaukee and he was listed as a 'plasterer' in the buildings industry. In the 1920, 1930 and 1940 Censuses, Henry and Molly lived at 829 Booth Street, Milwaukee. His occupation remained that of a mason/plasterer. They had three children: Hulda, born circa 1890; Walter, born circa 1892; Geo, born circa 1894.

As an interesting note, Theodore and Bertha Ramsthal lived at 710 Booth Street, Milwaukee for 30+ years. Did the two families know each other from their permanent residences on Booth Street?

Second Sale. Lot 3. The first owners of Lot 3 were Fred and Rose Engelmann. This was the second sale and is dated Sep 16, 1927. The details are shown on Vol 210, Page 318, #156441. As a result of the original Lot 4 not being wide enough on its own for a cottage, it was split between such that whomever owned Lot 3 would also own the south half of the old Lot 4 and whomever owned Lot 5 would also own the north half of the old Lot 4.

318

According to ancestry records, Fred Engelmann's legal name was Friedrich Peter Engelmann and was born Jul 23, 1886. I only found one record of his death which was Jan 19, 1953. Rose Engelmann was born Rose Neils on Oct 8, 1889. Other records for her were scarce. I could not find a date of death for her. They had one son, Alvin H. Engelmann who was born on May 1, 1909 and died in 1988. According to federal census data, Fred was a butcher all his adult life and owned his own shop in 1930. Both Fred and Rose are listed on the 1950 Census with an interesting twist. Both are listed as Divorced but living in the same dwelling. Rose is shown as Head of Household and Fred was shown as a lodger. According to records at the Register of Deeds office, Rose had executed a Quit Claim deed of Lot 3 on the peninsula to Fred on Jun 30, 1943. Also, in the 1950 Census, Rose was employed as an Inspector at a glove factory. Fred was still a butcher. Their son Alvin H. Engelmann, as a young man in the 1930 Census, was a truck driver in the Meat Market industry, apparently for his father. Alvin later became a FireFighter for the City of Milwaukee and retired from a long career with the City.

Third Sale. Lot 5. Charles F. Engelmann and his wife Martha (Moschgan) Engelmann, purchased Lot 5 on Sep 26, 1927. This was the third sale on the peninsula and just 10 days later than Fred and Rose Engelmann's purchase. Charles and Fred were brothers with Charles being 15 years senior to Fred. Vol 210, Page 317, #156460 records the transaction.

Approximately six weeks after their purchase, Charles and Martha signed, on Nov 4, 1927, a right of way document authorizing The Milwaukee Electric Railway and Light Company to run overhead wires to their lot. Milwaukee City Directories dated: 1895, 1908, 1915, and 1928 all listed the Engelmanns as living at 1332 Fond du Lac Avenue, Milwaukee. These City Directories listed Charles as a bookkeeper and the 1920 Federal Census further disclosed 'Sash and Door' in the column labeled: Industry.

One person's Ancestry.com tree shows Charles' residence in 1935 as: Nagauicka *(probably a typo)*, Waukesha, Wisconsin. There was no source document however. Were they using the peninsula as their permanent residence? Perhaps.

In the 1940 Federal Census, Charles Engelmann was shown to be living at 2425 Fond du Lac Avenue as a boarder with his younger brother Fred Engelmann and Fred's wife, Rose Engelmann. The Census also listed that Charles was divorced. Perhaps the answer to the 1935 residence question, Charles and Martha had separated and he was using the cottage as his permanent address. He died on Jun 7, 1947 at the age of 76.

The Engelmann's had three daughters: Florence (1897-1983); Myrtle (1900-1921); and Evelyn (1902-1992).

Fourth Sale. Lot 7. The fourth and last sale on the peninsula was to Frank Geiger, Mar 29, 1928, Vol 212, Page 174, # 157307.

I did some ancestry research and found there were multiple Frank Geigers in Wisconsin. By process of elimination via Ancestry.com, I found that the first owner of Lot 7, was Frank Xavier Geiger (1885-1956). According to a draft registration card signed on Apr 25, 1942, Frank Xavier Geiger listed his address as Rt. 1, Nashota, WI and that he was born on Mar 2, 1885. Also on Ancestry.com, the Wisconsin, US Death Records show that Frank died on Nov 24, 1956.

The 1950 Federal Census shows that Frank (age 65) was living at Ramsthal's Subdivision as Head of Household. Also living at that residence was Fred H. Geiger (age 38), son, and Fred's wife Irma (age 34) and their son Jerry Geiger, age 3.

An interesting document, Vol 864, Page 176, Doc #532339, showed that Fred H. Geiger (the son), sought approval through the County Court of Waukesha County, that he was acting in his capacity of <u>Administrator with will annexed of said estate</u> (for Frank X. Geiger, deceased). The purpose was to obtain the court's approval to sell Lot 7 and this document was dated Jul 26, 1960. Thus, Fred and his family continued to live on the peninsula for an additional four years after the death of his father before selling the house. I recall from my childhood days (in the 1950s) when visiting my Wisconsin relatives, that the Geigers' house was the only one of the five that had been converted into a year round house. This photo of the Geiger house in the background is a frozen frame from the Ramsthal family video and the date is circa 1931. Unfortunately, this frame does not show anything higher than the first floor windows of the cottage on Lot 7. I do remember that the Geiger house was larger than the other five. Bertha is seen here having just picked some flowers.

Lot 6. There was not much in the way of documentation about the Ramsthal <u>cottage</u> on Lot 6. A question in my mind remained: When did Theodore and Bertha build their cottage? After researching the sale of the other four lots, I have been able to reasonably conclude that the Ramsthal cottage showed up between 1927 and 1931.

I am using the words 'showed up' because the following two photos show that the cottage was not built on-site. Rather, it was constructed somewhere other than the peninsula and then brought to the peninsula. Easier said than done. The width of the peninsula is not wide enough to transport a fully constructed cottage on land. In addition to trees, there were already three structures that were shown on the March 1927 survey. The answer is shown in the photo below. Someone's light bulb went on in their head...Let's wait until the channel is frozen over and bring a fully built cottage across the iced-over channel. Sure. Sounds like a plan to me.

As can be seen, the Charles Englemann cottage (Lot 5 in the background) is complete with an outdoor table in the front. This photograph seems to prove that the earliest the Ramsthal cottage's arrival could have been would be the winter of 1927-1928. Secondly, this cottage for Lot 6 was delivered via a fairly complex underpinning of support for the weight of the house. It also appears that some form of rails were employed to push or pull the house across the iced over channel. This view shows the back of the cottage. Notice also, the bog that appears at the bottom of the photo.

The second photo shows the front of the cottage. We do not know who the man is. It is certainly conceivable that this is Theodore but we are not certain. What we also do not know is: how did the house get from this point to its final resting place?

How much heaving and hoeing went on to push or pull the cottage over. Men and/or horses? We do not know. Had the foundation already been dug out to accept the structure? Notice the trees in the first photo above. Is the foundation just to the left of the trees? Apparently it was.

In the spring of 2024, I received a family video from my cousin, Jenny Jensen as she went through some of her family's memorabilia. The entire video (there is no audio), which lasts 8:43 minutes, covers the time period starting in 1931 and then (at 2:11) skips to 1934-35. I went through and created various freeze frames for inclusion in this book to provide a better visual of life back in the 1930s. They will be presented in roughly the same sequence as the video. One surprise was finding an icebox used for refrigeration.

In the previous two photos, the author's mother, Patricia Jean McNamara Smith (1924-1985), is helping her aunt, Leona Ramsthal Eichfeld, put glass milk bottles in the icebox. *Author's note: I am estimating that my mother looked to be approximately 7 years old in this shot. If that is accurate, then this video was shot in 1931. Kenneth W. Eichfeld (1904-1940), husband of Leona Ramsthal Eichfeld, enjoyed a successful hobby in photography and video. Ken would have most likely been the photographer/videographer.* The author met with his aunt, Joan Brenkus Jensen, and her daughter, Jennifer Jensen, in May 2024. Joan remembers that the location of the icebox was also where an outdoor table was located and used to clean fish after being caught. The photo below of the fish cleaning table was taken in 1985 of the side yard of Lot 6. What was missing in this photo was the pump that was used to supply water (well water) when gutting and cleaning the fish. The well water below the surface always provided cold great tasting water. It is unknown when the conversion of an icebox into a table occurred.

Since these cottages were mostly set up to be used only in the spring, summer and perhaps, early fall, maintenance of the cottage and its grounds was always challenging. In the next photo, we find Theodore cleaning out weeds and other 'who knows what' stuff from the channel in the back of the cottages. I was very glad to see what his scow looked like. The second photograph seems to be in the channel behind Lot 7. Note that there is still a fair amount of bog in the channel.

If Theodore was not working on his scow, there was always some bailing that would have to be done.

Compare the photo below to the sepia colored photograph on page 8. Is it possible that the cameraman for this frame of the video reel be standing reasonably close to where the cameraman was in the earlier picture? If so, much of the bog would have been displaced over some period of time.

A front view of the cottage on Lot 6 (frame from the video in 1931) shows Theodore on the front corner on the right hand side of the photo. Going back to what year the pre-assembled cottage was towed to its present location, the front porch had been added at some point prior to this 1931 video.

This is the very wide and open side yard between Lot 6 on the right and Lot 5 on the left as of 1931.

A good look at the front of the cottage on Lot 5 taken while standing in the front yard of Lot 6.

While there is some overlap, the following two still frames show a decent panorama looking north from Lot 6.

The outhouse was in good working order.

A summer cottage would not be complete without a requisite outdoor facility. The Ramsthals had a two-door outhouse…no waiting. This photo was taken in 1987 but still looked pretty much exactly the way it did in the 1930s - 1950s. It is not known when the wooden screen was put up. I do not remember the wooden screen being there in the 1950s.

For the rest of the decade of the 1930s, there was not much associated with the cottages on the peninsula itself other than Rights of Way granted to The Milwaukee Electric Railway and Light Company.

On Feb 1, 1937, Bertha Koepp Ramsthal passed away. For reasons unknown, there were no submittals to the Register of Deeds to effect the transfer of her one-half ownership of the cottage and land to Theodore as the surviving spouse…until 1944. Even then, in 1944, the real estate paperwork only happened because Theodore Ramsthal, himself, passed away on Oct 2, 1943. Their combined estate went to the probate court on Jun 15, 1944. The value of the cottage and the land it sat on was appraised to be worth $1,800.00 at the time of probate.

Toward the end of 1939, the Charles F. Engelmanns divorced. Perhaps, as a result of the divorce proceedings, Martha became the owner of Lot 5 on Dec 27, 1939. The transfer of ownership is recorded in Vol 277, Page 639, # 231069 and shown below.

Roughly nine months later on Aug 29, 1940, Martha Engelmann sold Lot 5 to Maurice J. and Ella (a/k/a Eleanore) Hoyer as shown in Vol 278, page 142, # 235371.

142

Martha Engelmann .... To .... Maurice J. Hoyer + Wife : "Spir Jr

WARRANTY DEED—Vol. 278   STATE OF WISCONSIN—FORM No. 1

NUMBER

235371

This Indenture, Made this _29th_ day of _August_ A. D., 19 _40_,

between _Martha Engelmann_

part _y_ of the first part, and

Maurice J. Hoyer and Ella Hoyer, his wife, or the survivor
of either

part _ies_ of the second part.

WITNESSETH, That the said part _y_ of the first part, for and in consideration of the sum of

One ($1.00) Dollar and other goods and valuable consideration

to _her_ in hand paid by the said part _ies_ of the second part, the receipt whereof is hereby confessed and acknowledged, ha _s_ given, granted, bargained, sold, remised, released, aliened, conveyed and confirmed, and by these presents do _es_ give, grant, bargain, sell, remise, release, alien, convey and confirm unto the said part _ies_ of the second part, _their_ heirs and assigns forever, the following described real estate, situated in the County of Waukesha and State of Wisconsin, to-wit:

Lot Five (5) and the North One-half (N. ½) of Lot Four (4) in the Plat of
Ramsthals Nagawicka Lake Subdivision, as recorded in the office of
the Register of Deeds for Waukesha County, being a part of the South
One-half (S ½) of the Southwest Quarter (S.W.¼) of Section Eight (8),
Town Seven (7) North, of Range Eighteen (18) East.

As part of the consideration, the said grantee, her heirs and assigns
is given a space of 10 x 18 feet on Lot One (1) for a garage, it to be
placed only on the south side of said lot, the place for the same to
be designated by said grantor; provided, however, that the garage is
being built of metal on the sides, and the said grantee, her heirs
and assigns pay one-fifth of the taxes for said lot One. In case
any violation of any of said provisions be made the said privilege is
forfeited to the same extent as if the same had never been granted.

Revenue Stamps
$2.20 Canceled

TOGETHER with all and singular the hereditaments and appurtenances thereunto belonging or in any wise appertaining; and all the estate, right, title, interest, claim or demand whatsoever, of the said part _y_ of the first part, either in law or equity, either in possession or expectancy of, in and to the above bargained premises, and their hereditaments and appurtenances.

TO HAVE AND TO HOLD the said premises as above described with the hereditaments and appurtenances, unto the said part _ies_ of the second part, and to _their_ heirs and assigns FOREVER.

AND THE SAID _Martha Engelmann_

for _her_ heirs, executors and administrators, do _es_ covenant, grant, bargain and agree to and with the said part _ies_ of the second part, _their_ heirs and assigns, that at the time of the ensealing and delivery of these presents _she is_ well seized of the premises above described, as of a good, sure, perfect, absolute and indefeasible estate of inheritance in the law, in fee simple, and that the same are free and clear from all incumbrances whatever, _____

and that the above bargained premises in the quiet and peaceable possession of the said part _ies_ of the second part, _their_ heirs and assigns, against all and every person or persons lawfully claiming the whole or any part thereof, _she_ will forever WARRANT AND DEFEND.

IN WITNESS WHEREOF, the said part _y_ of the first part ha _s_ hereunto set _her_ hand and seal this _29th_ day of _August_ A. D., 19 _40_

Signed and Sealed in Presence of

Elsie Kozlowski
P. W. Witeck

Martha Engelmann (SEAL)
_____ (SEAL)
_____ (SEAL)
_____ (SEAL)

STATE OF WISCONSIN,
Milwaukee County. } ss.

Personally came before me, this _29th_ day of _August_ A. D., 19 _40_, the above named _Martha Engelmann_

to me known to be the person who executed the foregoing instrument and acknowledged the same.

Received for Record this _5th_ day of
September A. D., 19 _40_, at _8³⁵_ o'clock P.M.
Marie L. Lattner
Register of Deeds.
Deputy.

NOTARY SEAL

Marie F. Stenbeck
Notary Public, _Milwaukee_ County, Wis.
My Commission expires _Mar. 16_ A. D., 19 _41_

The Hoyers were the owners when my family would come up in the summers during the 1950s and into the early 1960s. Mr. Hoyer was always referred to 'as Old Man Hoyer' by my grandmother but we children were certainly not allowed to call him anything other than Mr. Hoyer. He owned a kayak and we would watch him paddle away from his front pier from time to time. Some ancestry research shows that Mr. Hoyer was one of the incorporators of E. P. Hoyer Company, a printing, engraving and bookbinding company, as reported in the Janesville Daily Gazette on Feb 6, 1914. Mr.

Hoyer was born in 1884 in Wisconsin but no city/county was listed. His wife, Ella passed away on Feb 2, 1958. They had one son, Irvin (1909-1976) who had five children. Interestingly, the 1910 Federal Census showed the Hoyers as living at 1084 Booth Street, Milwaukee. As mentioned previously, the Schumanns also lived on Booth Street in the 1920s and Theodore and Bertha lived many years at 710 Booth Street, Milwaukee. With three of the five early owners having lived on Booth Street, a pretty good case can be made that they knew each other prior to all having cottages at Ramsthal's Nagawicka Lake Subdivision.

After Ella Hoyer passed away, Mr. Hoyer filed a Certificate of Survivorship with the Milwaukee County Court as indicated in: Vol 766, pages 543-546, #477508. Within that document, it stated that the Hoyer's permanent residence was the Village of Shorewood, County of Milwaukee, Wisconsin. Mr. Hoyer would pass away on Jan 30, 1966.

1944

By 1944, both Theodore and Bertha Ramsthal had passed away (1937 and 1943 respectively). Concerning their estate, I visited the Waukesha County Register of Deeds office in May 2024. I found some answers in: Volume 356, Pages 200 - 210, Document # 265756. This one document provides answers to several questions concerning their estate.

- Certificate of Survivorship from the death of Bertha on Feb 1, 1937 to husband Theodore, pages 200 - 202.
- The date of (Theodore's and Bertha's) purchase of the peninsula under a warranty deed from Magdalena Kunz on Feb 23, 1912, page 201.
- This document references Vol 133, Page 486, and Document # 77655 as the source document for the original sale/purchase in 1912. *(Note: Armed with this new, fantastic piece of information, I went online at the Waukesha Register of Deeds website. After inputting the above Volume, Page and Document numbers, there were no results from my inquiry. I then re-entered multiple variations of volume numbers, page numbers and document numbers. All to no avail. Until I can discover the correct set of numbers to the original source document's above three categories, this Certificate of Survivorship document will remain the source document for the original purchase date and the seller.)*
- An additional legal matter mentioned in the Document # 265756 is Theodore Ramsthal's Last Will and Testament and associated paperwork that went to Probate Court in June 1944 for the settlement of Theodore's estate.

NOTE: Document # 265756. Only pages 200 - 202 are presented on the following pages which shows the date of the original sale to Theodore and Bertha.

While this document answered the question of when the purchase was executed, I did not find any documentation between the years 1912 through 1926. Did they occupy the land in the summer? Were the photographs dated in 1914 and 1916 related to the peninsula? The answers to these questions remain unknown as of the printing of this book in 2025.

VOL **356** PAGE **200**

STATE OF WISCONSIN   :   COUNTY COURT   :   MILWAUKEE COUNTY

- - - - - - - - - - - - - - - - - - -

In the Matter of the Survivorship
of THEODORE F. RAMSTHAL, in and to
the Real Estate of

            BERTHA RAMSTHAL,

                Deceased.

                       CERTIFICATE OF SURVIVORSHIP

- - - - - - - - - - - - - - - - - - - -

       Upon reading and filing the duly verified petition of
Eleanor Brenkus, and upon the testimony taken in open court, I,
the undersigned, Judge of the County Court of Milwaukee County,
do hereby find and certify:

       That the petition of Eleanor Brenkus respectfully shows
that she is a daughter of Theodore F. Ramsthal, deceased, who
died on October 2, 1943, in the City and County of Milwaukee,
State of Wisconsin.

       That at the time of his death the said Theodore Ramsthal,
deceased, was the surviving husband of Bertha Ramsthal, deceased;
that said Bertha Ramsthal died on February 1, 1937, and at the
time of her death was a resident of Milwaukee County.

       That at the time of the death of Bertha Ramsthal, the said
Theodore F. Ramsthal, the father of petitioner, and the said Bertha
Ramsthal were husband and wife and were the owners of the follow-
ing described real estate, to-wit:

            All that part of the North Sixty (60) acres
            of the South One half ($\frac{1}{2}$) of the Southwest
            Quarter ($\frac{1}{4}$) of Section Eight (8), Town Seven
            (7) North of Range Eighteen (18) East, bounded
            and described as follows, to-wit: Commencing
            at a point in the South line of said Sixty (60)
            acre tract Twenty one hundred thirty four (2134)
            feet East from the South West corner thereof;
            thence North at right angles Four hundred sixty
            two (462) feet to a stake; thence East, parallel
            to the South line of said Sixty (60 acre tract
            to a point in the West shore of Nagawicka Lake;
            thence South along the shore of said Lake to its
            intersection with the South line of said Sixty
            (60) acre tract; thence West along the South
            line of said Sixty (60) acre tract to the place
            of beginning, in the Town of Delafield.

Also a drive way along the South line of
above described premises sufficient in width
for a team to drive through with additional
room for passing over fifteen rods.

under a warranty deed from Magdalena Kunz of the Village of
Mukwonago, Waukesha County and State of Wisconsin, to the said
Theodore F. Ramsthal and wife, Bertha Ramsthal, of Milwaukee,
and State of Wisconsin, as husband and wife, dated February 23,
1912 and acknowledged February 23, 1912, and recorded in the
Office of the Register of Deeds for Waukesha County, Wisconsin,
February 28, 1912, in Volume 133 of Deeds on page 486, as Document
No. 77655.

That at the time of the death of Bertha Ramsthal, the said
Theodore F. Ramsthal, the father of petitioner, and the said
Bertha Ramsthal were husband and wife and were the owners of the
following described real estate, to-wit:

West thirty (30) feet of Lot Thirty-
two (32) of Barracks Woodland Park, in
North West one-quarter of Section Eight
(8), Town Seven (7) North, of Range
Eighteen (18) East.

under a quit claim deed from John Winkelmann and Clara Winkelmann,
his wife, to the said Theodore F. Ramsthal and Bertha Ramsthal,
his wife, as husband and wife, dated June 12, 1925 and acknowledged
June 12, 1925, and recorded in the Office of the Register of Deeds
for Waukesha County, Wisconsin, June 16, 1925, in Volume 192 of
Deeds on page 43 as Document No. 138552.

That the aforesaid real estate at the time has been appraised
in the matter of the Estate of Theodore F. Ramsthal, deceased,
File No. 235-159 by appraisers appointed by this Court to be worth
$1,800.00; that there has been a determination of inheritance tax
in said matter.

That by reason of the death of the said Bertha Ramsthal, her
interest in said real estate has ceased and terminated, and that
the said real estate is now freed from all right, title and interest
therein whatsoever of the said Bertha Ramsthal, and the title to

the whole thereof, by reason of her death, became absolutely

vested in the said Theodore F. Ramsthal, and that he is now

the lawful owner of said real estate, subject to any lien and

incumbrance, thereon.

That the inheritance tax has been paid.

Dated at Milwaukee, Wisconsin, this 15th day of June,

1944.

Executed in duplicate.

County Judge.

STATE OF WISCONSIN
MILWAUKEE COUNTY
COUNTY _____ COURT

In the Matter of the Survivorship of THEODORE F. RAMSTHAL,
in and to the Real Estate of

BERTHA RAMSTHAL,

Deceased.

CERTIFICATE OF SURVIVORSHIP

ORIGINAL COPY

REGISTER'S OFFICE

GAUER AND BUER
ATTORNEYS AT LAW
113 W. WISCONSIN AVENUE
MILWAUKEE, WIS.

Nine days after the previous document (Jun 15, 1944) was completed, Eleanor Brenkus executed a quit claim deed (on Lot 6) from her sister, Leona Ramsthal Eichfeld, on Jun 24, 1944. I was a little taken aback when I found this document. Eleanor and Leona were sisters and were co-inheritors of the Lot 6 cottage and land from their father, Theodore Ramsthal. Why would Leona give up her 50% ownership less than two weeks after their father's estate was settled in probate?

Then it hit me. Leona had been somewhat recently widowed, her husband Ken having passed away on Dec 9, 1940. She was now a single mother raising an 11 year old son without a husband to help with maintenance of the Nagawicka cottage. Leona never remarried and remained single for the rest of her life. Volume 355, pages 581 and 582, Document # 265758 of the quit claim deed are presented below.

1973

The Ramsthal family cottage was sold by my grandmother, Eleanor Ramsthal Brenkus to a couple who were long time family friends…Quinton and Marjorie (Marge) Sutton. This was recorded on Jul 13, 1973.

DOCUMENT NO. 047 IMAGE 147   TRANSFER   STATE BAR OF WISCONSIN — FORM 1
856974 $ 15.00   WARRANTY DEED

REGISTER'S OFFICE 856974
Waukesha Co. Wis. }   NO.

FEE

This Deed, made between **Eleanor Brenkus, A Widow**   RECEIVED FOR RECORD THE _16th_ DAY

JULY, A. D. 19**73** AT 2:33

——————————————————— Grantor O'CLOCK P. M. & RECORDED IN REEL **47**

and **Quintin H. Sutton and Marjorie K. Sutton,** OF RECORDS IMAGE _147_

His Wife

——————————————————— Grantee. *Michael J. Hasslinger*

REGISTER

Witnesseth, That the said Grantor for a valuable consideration

Mr. Lewis D. Houting

conveys to Grantee the following described real estate in **Waukesha** County. RETURN TO Vice Pres. & Cashier
State of Wisconsin: Marine Nat'l Bank–Waukesha
235 W. Broadway, Waukesha
Lots numbered One (1) and Six (6), in Ramsthal's Wisconsin 53186.
Nagawicka Lake Subdivision of part of the North Tax Key #
60 acres of the South One-half (1/2) of the South This is **not** homestead property.
West One-quarter (1/4) of Section numbered
Eight (8), in Township numbered Seven (7)
North, Range numbered Eighteen (18) East, in
the City of Delafield. Excepting the right
granted to Frank Geiger, Henry Schumann and
wife, Fred P. Engelmann and wife and Charles
F. Engelmann and wife, wherein they are given
a space of 10 x 18 feet on Lot numbered One (1)
for a garage to be placed only on the South side
of said Lot, the place for the same to be designated by Theodore F. Ramsthal and wife.

Together with all and singular the hereditaments and appurtenances thereunto belonging or in any wise appertaining:
And **Eleanor Brenkus, A Widow**
warrants that the title is good, indefeasible in fee simple and free and clear of encumbrances except **municipal and
zoning ordinances and recorded easements and building restrictions,
if any.**
and will warrant and defend the same.
Executed at **Waukesha, Wisconsin** this **13th,** day of **July** 19 **73.**

SIGNED AND SEALED IN PRESENCE OF   *Eleanor Brenkus* (SEAL)
Eleanor Brenkus

(SEAL)

(SEAL)

(SEAL)

Signatures of

authenticated this day of 19

Title: Member State Bar of Wisconsin or Other Party
Authorized under Sec. 706.06 viz.

STATE OF WISCONSIN }
Waukesha County. } ss.
Personally came before me, this **13th,** day of **July** 19 **73**
the above named **Eleanor Brenkus**

to me known to be the person S who executed the foregoing instrument and acknowledged the same.

THIS INSTRUMENT WAS DRAFTED BY   *Leone M. Smith*

Lewis D. Houting, Vice President   Leone M. Smith
and Cashier.
The use of witnesses is optional.   Notary Public, **Waukesha** County, Wis.
My commission (expires) (is) **November 14, 1976**
Names of persons signing in any capacity should be typed or printed below their signatures.

WARRANTY DEED   STATE BAR OF WISCONSIN   Wisconsin Legal Blank Company
FORM No. 1—1971   Milwaukee, Wis. (Job 30687)

Quinton H. Sutton was an engineer who studied at the Milwaukee School of Engineering (MSOE) which had been organized in 1903. Enrollment of MSOE was approximately 2,800 students in 1948. He and Majorie Jane Krohn married on Sep 11, 1948.

Quinton was an engineer at the RTE Corporation for 35 years. During that time, he was awarded two certificates for patents from the U. S. Patent & Trademark Office.

An interesting note on Marge Krohn Sutton occurred in the newspapers in February 1948 before she and Quinton married in September 1948.

Narrow Door Calls for Slim Receptionist

MILWAUKEE, Wis. (U.P.)—The Frank H. Bercker office is guaranteed a slim receptionist so long as it stays in the Grain Exchange building.

The door to the receptionist's office, one of the narrowest in Milwaukee, is slightly less than 18 inches wide.

Marjorie Krohn, present receptionist, gets in by turning sidewise.

I was looking for some information about Marge via Newspapers.com. It was interesting to find that this exact article appeared in **51 newspapers** in **24 states** between February and May, 1948.

I clipped this one that had been published by the Pomona Progress Bulletin, Pomona, California on Apr 26, 1948.

The Suttons made the following photographs when they were preparing to sell the cottage in 1995.

Front

Back

Chapter 4. Aerial Photography - Waukesha County

Aerial photograph: 1941 on top. Aerial photograph: 1950 on bottom.

Aerial photograph: 1963 on top. Aerial photograph: 1970 on bottom.

Aerial photograph: 1980 on top. Aerial photograph: 1990 on bottom.

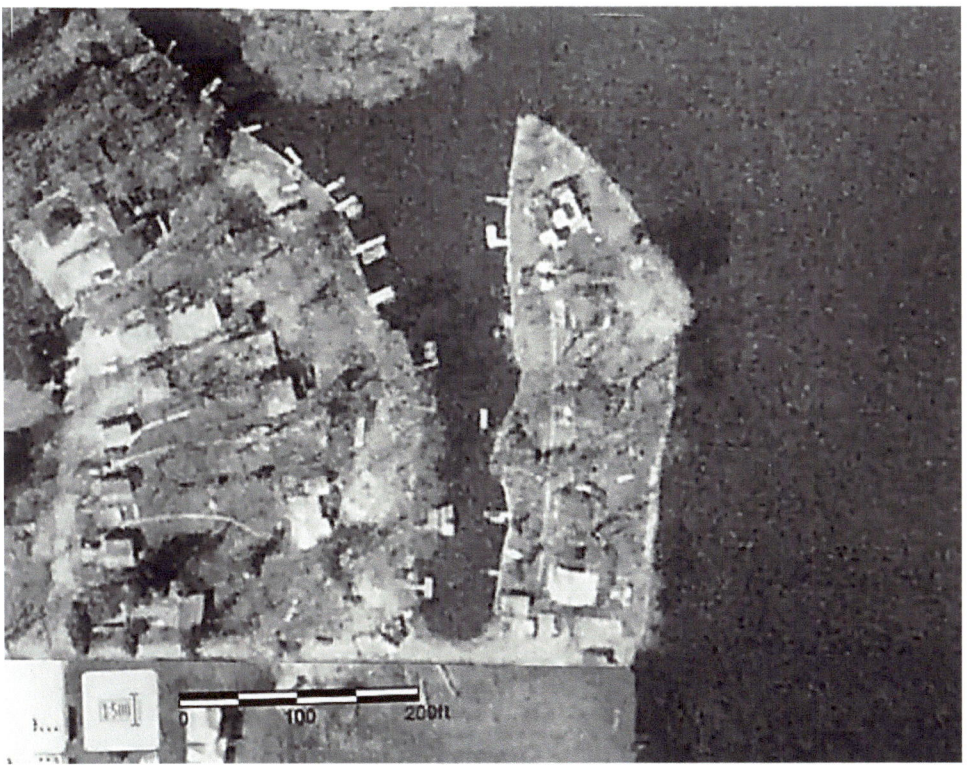

Aerial photograph: 1995 on top. Aerial photograph: 2000 on bottom.

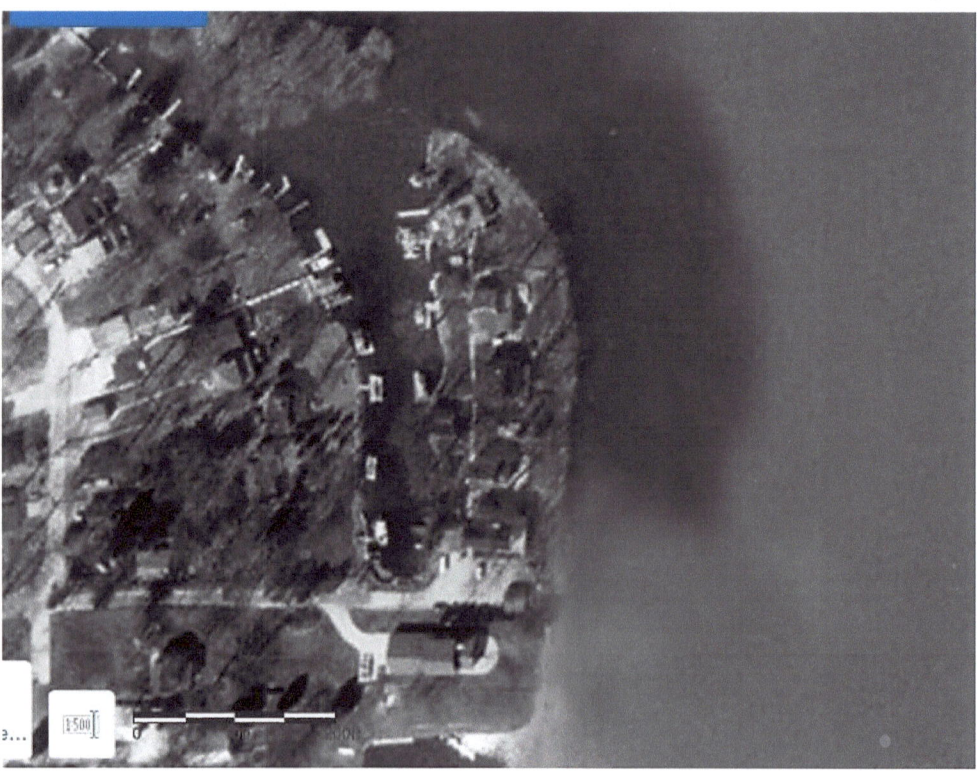

Chapter 5. Life and Times

1930s

The date of this photo is unknown but I am estimating it to be in the 1930s. I say that because the condition of the water and shoreline of the channel is pretty well defined. This would suggest that whatever bog had been back there was mostly or entirely gone by the late 1930s. I reference the reader back to the first survey conducted in 1927.

The location of the second photo appears to be taken while standing on Lot 6 and looking north onto the channel side of Lot 7. The condition of the boats looks pretty good so I am putting an educated guess that this is the 1930s to 1940s.

1940s

This photo shows Eleanor Brenkus, her daughter Joan Brenkus and her husband Louis Brenkus. Joan is holding her father's catch that day. Joan's best memory is that she was about 15 years old at the time. This would date the photo to be Summer of 1948. This fish is known within family lore as The Big Fish. I am certain that it became dinner that night. Louis would have the head mounted and it hung above the doorway going from the main room onto the front porch. It was removed from the cottage at some point after the sale to the Suttons.

Ah! The mounted Big Fish is displayed here. This is a zoomed-in photograph and looks larger and way more menacing than the photograph listed above. It was the largest fish Grandpa (Louis) ever caught.

The following photo was taken in the summer of 1949. I am the baby sitting in my Aunt Joan Brenkus's lap. Joan was 16 in this photograph. My brother Bryan, sitting on Joan's left, would be age 4 in this photo. The young woman on the left is Joan's friend, Lois Luedtke.

This was taken on the pier on the Channel side of Lot 6. The shoreline of the channel in this photograph is more built up compared to the sepia colored photograph shown on page 55.

Another photo from the summer of 1949 was taken in the front yard of Lot 6 looking south at the cottage on Lot 5. The cottage on Lot 5 was originally a much lighter color as shown earlier around 1931. It was a darker brown by the late 1940s. It is one of the few that shows the Lot 5 cottage as it looked in 1949. My mother, Patricia Smith (1924-1985) is holding me and my brother Bryan is sitting on the bench.

1950s

These family photos are from the 1950s. This little swimming pier was roughly 75 yards almost directly in front of Lot 6, maybe slightly to the left. I refer the reader back to page 2 in the section of this book titled **Background.** This aerial photograph taken in 2022 shows an elongated sandbar running north and south. The swimming pier would have been in the sandbar area. This pier had to be put up each year for the summer months and then taken down at the end of the summer. Each corner had to be 'set' in the sand and then connected to each other. The flat boards would have been nailed to the cross members that connected the four corners. The process began with Joan jumping into the water from the boat and would use her feet to 'locate' an indention in the sand from the previous year's posts. Her father, Louis Brenkus would have then taken the post from the boat and placed it in the slightly hollowed out sand. He would use his sledgehammer to pound it into place. Once the four posts had been set, he would attach the side pieces to the corner posts and then nail the flat boards onto the side boards. Little did we realize the efforts that went into that little 5 foot square pier until we were grown. That process was reversed at the end of each summer due to the lake freezing over each winter.

This photo is from the summer of 1953.

Joan Brenkus, age 20. The author, Jim Smith, age 5, is jumping off the pier. Bryan Smith, age 8, is in the water.

This photo is also dated 1953 and shows the front of the cottage on Lot 6. Our family had two row boats. One was store-bought and the second was made by my grandfather, Louis Brenkus. The boat in this photo is the one he made. One person I recognize from this photo is the woman standing mid-way between the shore and the cottage…in a mid-dark dress. This is Eleanor Ramsthal Brenkus, aka Grandma. The second person that looks familiar is the woman standing at the foot of the steps to the cottage. That looks like my mother, Patricia M. Smith, solely based on the way she is standing. The last one I recognize is the man kneeling holding onto a young boy(?). That is Grandpa, Louis Brenkus. I do not know who the people are that are standing on the pier, but probably family members.

Using the above photo as a backdrop, fast forward five years to 1958. My brother, Bryan then 13 and I then 10 had swum from this shore pier out to the swimming pier shown previously…to go swimming. We normally would row one of the boats out to the pier, but for some reason we swam out. Perhaps Bryan dared me to swim out to the pier. I probably hesitated, and the dare became a 'double-dog dare'. Well, everyone knows that you cannot turn down a double-dog dare. The first 20+ yards of the lake bottom was very murky and mushy. If you stepped on the lake bottom, it was very squishy.

Nevertheless, Bryan and I were swimming back to the shore when we looked up to see Grandma standing at the end of the pier on the shore. We were still about 20 feet away from the pier. In her hand was a pointed shovel. She was calling out loudly: "You boys hurry up! Hurry up!"

We did not know what kind of trouble we had gotten into…but we hurried up appropriately. We climbed onto the pier and Grandma quickly shuffled us off the pier onto the front yard.

Unbeknownst to us, a snake had been following us from the swimming pier towards the shore. She instructed Bryan to get a hoe from behind the house while she tried to get the snake onto the ground with her shovel. She was successful in doing that, but the pointed end of the shovel was making Grandma's task of beheading the snake more difficult. Bryan was helping to keep the snake from moving but ultimately it slithered back into the water.

No one was permitted outside the cottage for the rest of the afternoon. When Grandpa showed up from work, Bryan and I ran to the parking lot to apprise him of our exciting run-in with the snake. At the same time, and as luck would have it, the snake erred in trying to get back onto land to nurse its wounds of almost having lost its head. That turned out to be a fatal mistake as Grandpa successfully completed the task of separating the head from the body of the snake. At that time, Grandpa said that he thought the snake was poisonous.

Needless to say, no one was ever permitted to swim out to the swimming pier again.

Bryan and I would fish from the front pier starting in the mid-1950s. I remember we would catch mostly brim, perch and sunfish. If you caught 'em, you had to gut 'em and clean 'em. Grandma or our mother would fry them and that was our meat for the night. Bryan and I were full fledged hunters and gatherers. I do not remember ever seeing anyone fishing in the channel. The water back there was pretty crummy back then. Remember, there were only outhouses on the peninsula until much later. A sewer easement for Lot 6 did not occur until Nov 7, 1978 according to Vol 372, pages 401-404, Document # 1102380.

Let's move back to the summer of 1954. This photo shows us in our store-bought boat. As you look at the boat, I am on the left in the front seat and Bryan is on the right. Our sister Susan is sitting behind us. The young boy sitting directly behind me was Bruce Krueger. Grandpa is in the back on the left. The woman sitting next to him was Gerri Perenchio, a friend of Joan's.

By this time, Bryan, then 9, learned how to operate the outboard motor that went onto this boat. It was an Evinrude with a whopping 8 horsepower. Bryan and I would go north from the cottage and follow the shoreline. I remember going through multiple channels and small islands with only vegetation, i.e., no cottages. Those were the bogs that had been around for close to 100 years. A photo of a 1948 model Evinrude is shown on the next page.

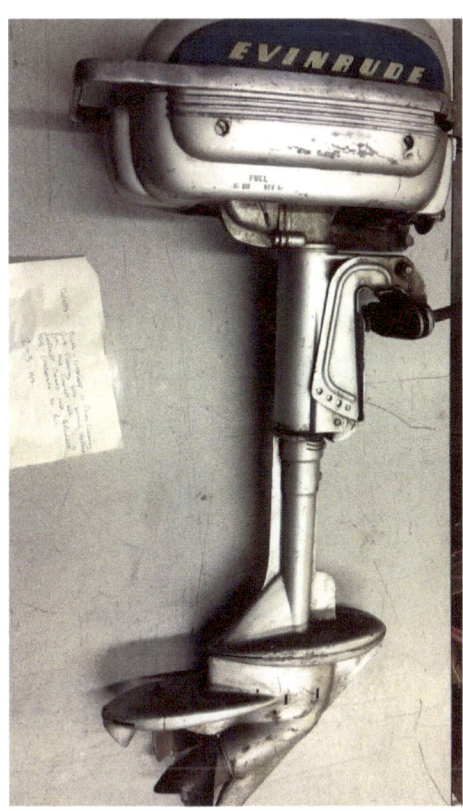

Circa 1995. This photograph shows Marge Sutton, then owner of the cottage on Lot 6, and Paiboon Pairin, husband of cousin Jenny Jensen. The photographer would have been standing close to the right front corner of the porch. The cast iron stove was still in place. The fish hanging above the doorway behind Marge is different from the 'Big Fish' that Grandpa caught.

A second photo, also taken in 1995, shows Jenny with her daughter, Siri, and the door of the front porch. The front and rear views of the cottage are also shown here.

Notice a nice view of The Geiger Cottage on Lot 7 as of 1995. In looking at the pic of Jenny and Siri, note the hand braided rugs on the floor. Eleanor made several such rugs over time from old wool clothing. I know the Jensen and the Smith families both had some of the hand braided rugs.

The next two photographs were taken in May 2024 when I came up from Tennessee to do research for this book. I am standing in the middle of the front yard of Lot 6 and snapped a photo looking north and one looking south from the shoreline. The object(s) of these two photos are 'the rocks' along the shore line. There's a story behind some of these rocks. In the 1950s, when our family would be in Wisconsin, Grandpa would take my brother, Bryan, and me and we went 'rock hunting'. We would leave our grandparents house in Wauwatosa and go out Bluemound Road on our way to Nagawicka Lake. We would stop periodically and pick up medium sized rocks alongside the shoulder of Bluemound Road and load them into the trunk of his 1950 Plymouth 2-door sedan. We would then 're-home' those rocks to the shoreline in front of our cottage. We would do this several times. The trunk of that car did not hold that many rocks at any one time. I wonder whether or not any child labor laws were broken. Just sayin'.

The following two photos were also taken in May 2024 looking at a 45 degree angle to the right and left while standing on the front lawn of Lot 6.

Two other maps I have purchased are shown here. This one is dated 1967.

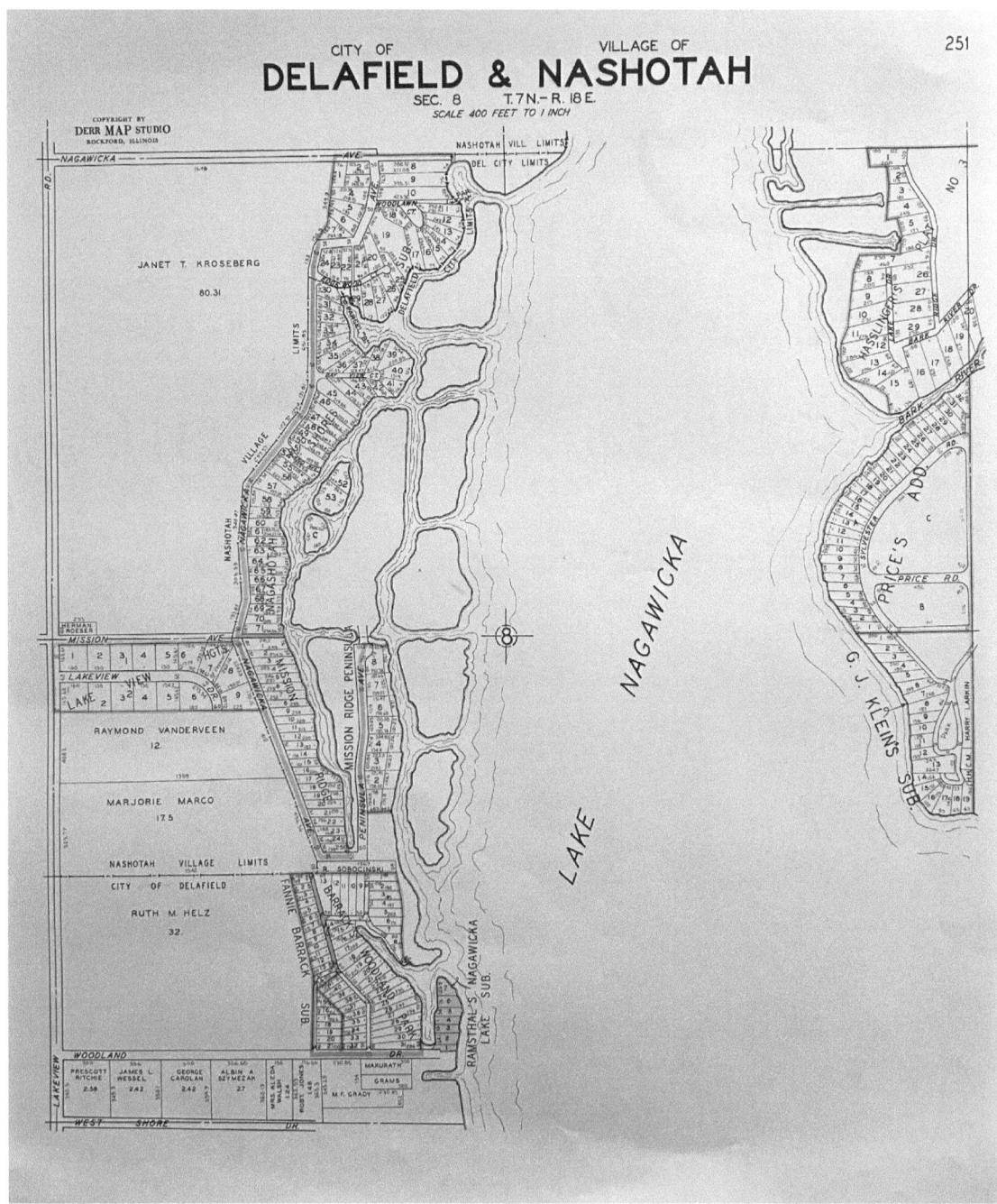

The land pieces that are blank indicate that they would still be considered bog…and hence, not buildable, from the standpoint of being able to construct a cottage/home.

This map is dated 1973.

This photo of Lot 6 is dated May 2024 and is used with permission of the current owners. The core of the original cottage can be identified on the right hand side. The second floor originally had two windows. When remodeling and additions occurred, the two windows were converted into one wider window.

These next photos come from the family video mentioned earlier in this book. I was trying to present them in a panoramic sequence.

Miscellaneous Photos and Information

The following is presented as additional information about Nagawicka Lake but not necessarily about the Peninsula.

From family photographs, Theodore Ramsthal in this photograph circa 1890s? He is seated on the front row holding a Bandoneon. He was born in 1870 and by his appearance in this photo could have been in his 20s. Location is unknown.

A bandoneon (sometimes spelled bandonion, or bandonium) was an instrument similar to an accordion. An internet photo shown below provides a closer view of the instrument.

The photo below is dated August 26, 1914, was taken at a park that had the name South Park written on the back. Research has not revealed whether South Park was located at Nagawicka Lake or Delafield, WI.

The next two photographs below are dated Aug 1916. Locations and names are unknown.

This photo is blurry but also dated Aug 1916. Based on the background, this location could be somewhere on the Peninsula…or maybe closer to shallow areas in Delafield.

The next four photos are all dated 1916 and show Southshore Park as the location.

The following four are all dated: Week of Aug 24, 1914 but no location was written down.

The photograph below could *possibly* have been taken on the Peninsula.

The week of Aug 24, 1914 but no names or locations.

There are two photographs showing Theodore at The Clubhouse. According to Joan B. Jensen, she remembers this was located on the north end of Nagawicka. There is a lot of bog still around the middle of the north end, so perhaps this building was located a little to the west towards Nashota. She was unsure of the purpose other than as a gathering spot for the men (perhaps to down a beer or two). Theodore is the third from the left and appears to be holding a pipe. The photo is undated but Joan's best guess was the mid-1920's.

This second photo of The Clubhouse was possibly taken at the same time frame but shows the building in its entirety.

Theodore is second from the left in this photograph.

Appendix

I have added this additional information for all the ancestry nerds out there. How did a man (the author) born and raised in Nashville, Tennessee have such an interest in Nagawicka Lake?

In the section titled **Background**, I made the reference that I am descended from Eleanor Ramsthal Brenkus. She was my maternal grandmother.

Eleanor was married twice, first to Leo Patrick McNamara and then to Louis F. Brenkus. From the first marriage came my mother, Patricia Jean McNamara. Leo and Eleanor married in 1922 and my mother was born from this union in May 1924. At some point after my mother was born, Leo and Eleanor split up. Eleanor and Patsy (as she was called as a child) moved in with her parents (Theodore and Bertha Ramsthal) sometime between 1925 and 1931. On July 18, 1931, Eleanor married Louis Brenkus. From this second marriage came Joan Louise Brenkus who was born in September 1933. Pat and Joan would thus be half-sisters. They lived in Wauwatosa…a part of greater Milwaukee.

Now, let's go to my father's side of this story. My father was Eugene (Gene) H. Smith. He was born and raised in Nashville, son of Brantley and Christine Priest Smith. Gene was the third of five children.

This article was printed on Aug 2, 1939, in the Nashville Banner. Father (Eugene) and (his younger brother) Billy were going to Dayton, Ohio to visit their older brother Brantley and Mrs. Smith (aunt Jessie).

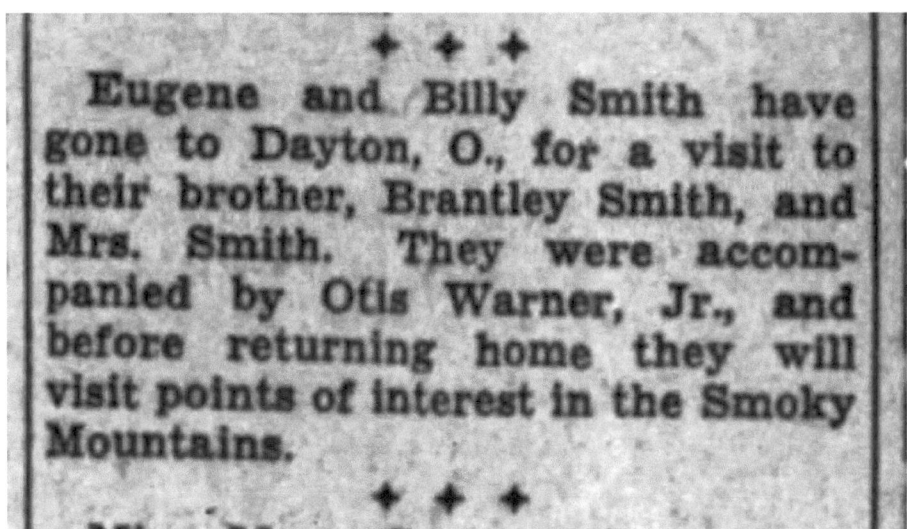

Eugene and Billy Smith have gone to Dayton, O., for a visit to their brother, Brantley Smith, and Mrs. Smith. They were accompanied by Otis Warner, Jr., and before returning home they will visit points of interest in the Smoky Mountains.

On their way home (to Nashville), they would stop in the Smoky Mountains. Which they did.

As destiny would have it, the Louis Brenkus family, (Louis, Eleanor, Patsy and Joan) would leave Milwaukee that first or second week of August 1939. Destination, Great Smoky Mountain Park. Keep in mind that World War II would start in less than one month on September 1, 1939.

The Great Smoky Mountain National Park (a.k.a., The Smokies) was established in 1926 and would continue to be improved and enlarged over several decades. Gatlinburg, Tennessee is a very popular tourist city in the Smokies but would not be incorporated until 1945. That said, hotels were few in number in the 1930s. According to family history, The Woodland Hotel was, perhaps, the only hotel in that general area.

Back to my story. Eugene, Billy and their friend, Otis Warner, stopped at a scenic overlook within the Smokies. The Brenkus' family also stopped at this same scenic overlook at the same time. Both groups got back into their respective cars and then "happened" to stop at a second overlook. Then a third, fourth and fifth. By this time, the two groups were waving to each other as they stopped to enjoy the sights.

By further providence, both groups just "happened" to stay at the Woodland Hotel. At this point, Father had obtained my mother's name, address and telephone number. Smooth talker, that Eugene. They would communicate via letters, some phone calls (long distance, of course), and a few visits from Nashville to Wauwatosa. Our father was a life insurance underwriter working at a large insurance company in Nashville, The National Life and Accident Insurance Company. The Company would put out a monthly newsletter (8 ½" x 11") with multiple pages. Each issue would have little stories about various employees and mention promotions, new additions to the family, etc. One such issue that I found, dated sometime in the summer of 1940, published a blurb that said: "Eugene Smith, Underwriting, has gone to Wisconsin to go 'dear' hunting."

After the Pearl Harbor bombing on December 7, 1941, Father entered the U.S. Army Air Corps in February 1942 and saved enough leave time to marry my mother in October 1943 in Milwaukee. They would later be stationed at Kearns Air Force Base, Salt Lake City, Utah where my brother, Bryan, would be born.

The Smith family would return to Nashville after he was discharged in February 1946. I arrived in 1948 followed by my sister, Susan, in 1950.

Oh, wait! I forgot to mention that back in 1939, at their first meeting, Father was 26. Mother was, um, 15! At the time of their marriage in 1943, they were 30 and 19. Nice and legal. Whew!

Each summer in the late 1940s, 1950s and into the 1960s, in mid-June, our mother and we three children would board the train called The Dixie Flyer around 7:00 p.m. and would arrive in Chicago around 8:00ish the following morning. Bench seating only…no berths.

The Dixie Flyer was a passenger train connecting Chicago to states in the southeast traveling the "Dixie Route" and serving Evansville, Indiana; Nashville, Tennessee; and Atlanta.

I did some sleuthing and discovered the following poster.

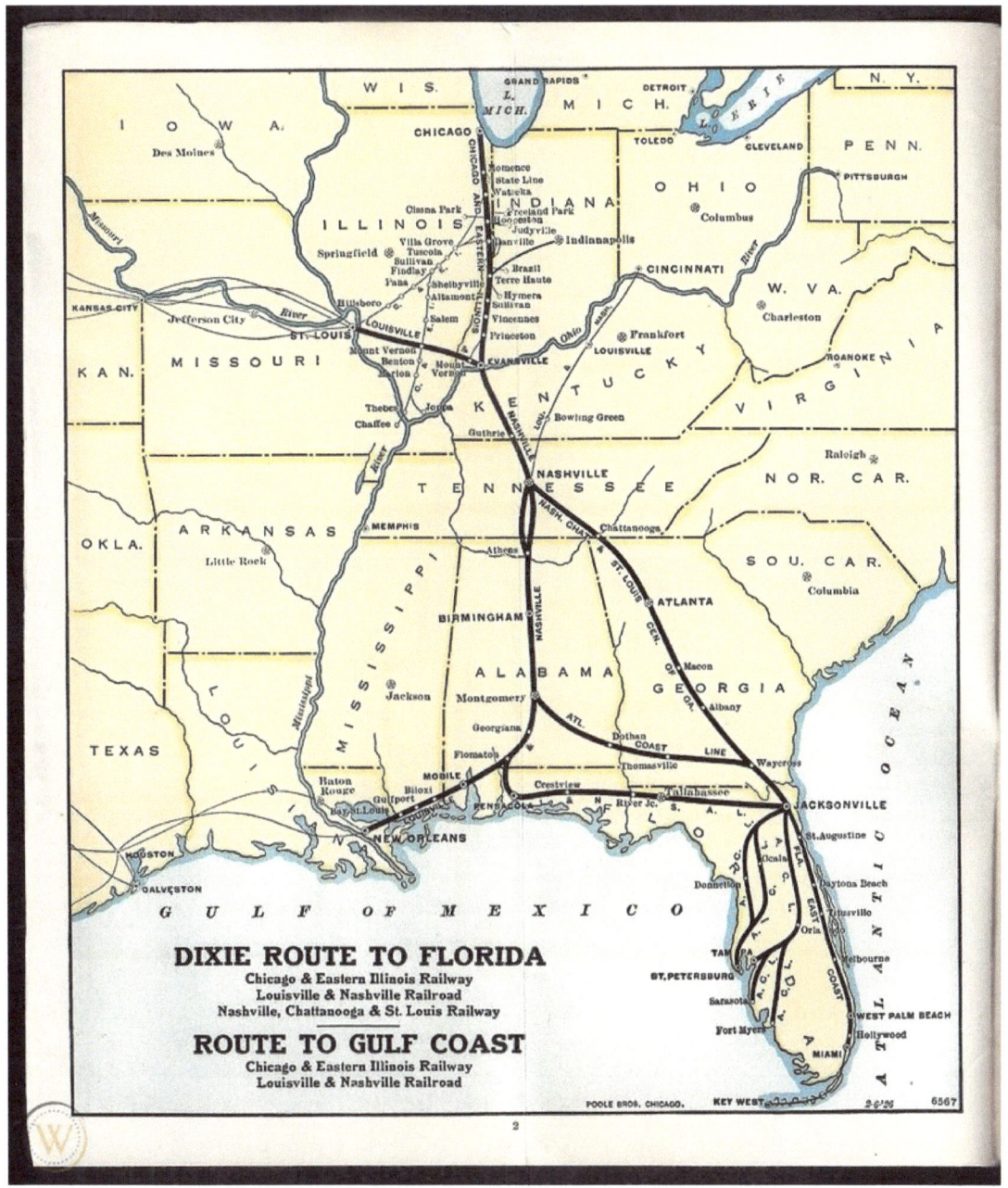

Louis and Eleanor (Grandpa and Grandma) would pick us up and we would spend the day sightseeing in Chicago before heading to Milwaukee. We would spend approximately two months in Milwaukee before heading back home. On weekends, our greater family: my grandparents, the Smiths and the Jensens (my aunt Joan had married a Jim Jensen and they had five children: Jody, Jill, Jenny, Jamie and John) would go 'out to the lake'...Nagawicka Lake, Lot 6.

Father got a reprieve from parental duties for six weeks or so and would drive up to spend two weeks in August in Wisconsin. The five of us would drive home in the family wagon in mid-August. No air conditioning. No radio, either. Radios cost money, you know.

The Ramsthal cottage in the 1950s was slightly different from the 1930s and early 1940s. Inside the back porch door, in a small kitchen, was a pump handle for well water. Most likely piped over from the outdoor pump handle about 20 feet away. As I recall, there was an electric stove at that point as well as a medium sized refrigerator.

The refrigerator would have had maybe a 12" x 12" open section for a freezer. Non self-deicing type. We had to chip away the built up frozen condensation every so often. The well water was always very cold and tasted great.

During the 50s up to the early 60s, everyone used the outhouse. The outhouse had two-doors. No waiting. We used a chamber pot during the night. We used a chamber pot during the night.

There were two trees close to the lot line next to Lot 5 that were big enough and the right length to put up a cloth hammock. The 'rockee' was entitled to a certain number of swings before changing places to become the 'rocker'.

As the two oldest of the grandchildren, Bryan and I fished on the front pier. I recall that we mostly caught sunfish, bream and perch. Standard operating procedure was that the person who caught the fish would throw them into a bucket filled with water. Once we (Bryan and I) caught enough, we would take the bucket to the outdoor wooden stand (where the outdoor icebox) was located.

If any fish were still alive, after swimming around in circles, we would bonk them on the head with the descaler tool to finish them off. We would then cut the head off; descale, gut 'em, and remove (hopefully all) the bones.

We would then turn our catch over to my mother, aunt Joan, or to Grandma to fry them up. Bryan and I earned our Hunter - Gatherer badges.

I remember that the large room downstairs (maybe 20' x 20') had a relatively large table for eating. There was a lone light socket in the middle of the ceiling for one bulb. Also in the room was a wood burning cast iron stove. The stove is now gone but the now covered up hole in the wall for the exhaust is still visible. Joan's recollection of the stove was that it was enameled iron, stood taller and was square shaped. There was no burner plate on top. My own recollection is that it was used for heating the room. A regular cooking stove was located in the small kitchen. Grandpa would brew a pot of coffee daily and leave it on the wood burning stove...to keep it reasonably warm. He would have started a fire in the stove on a chilly morning. The coffee pot would remain on top and he would drink a cup periodically during the day. Cold. Grandpa told me once that he actually liked it cold, which, by definition, would also mean 'strong'. I think I took a sip of the now cold coffee once one afternoon. That was the first time I noticed hair on my chest. Think I was about 8.

In the mid-1950's, as Bryan and I got a little older, he and I were permitted to take the 'store bought' boat (with an 8 HP Evinrude motor). We would motor north along the shoreline on the west side of Nagawicka where the bogs were still very evident. There were many little channels that we would explore in this new section of the lake. As I remember, this area was relatively unpopulated versus the southwest section of Nagawicka, closer to Delafield, WI. We felt so grown up.

As life happens, we grew up. As a family, we probably stopped coming up in the summers around 1961. Bryan turned 16 that year and started working summer jobs back home in Nashville. I did the same thing in 1964 although I remember my mother and I drove up to Milwaukee that summer. Just the two of us. We only stayed a week, maybe two weeks. We came back and I started working summer jobs. The money that both Bryan and I earned during high school summers went into our college fund. Folding money (i.e. date money) came from cutting grass and other jobs.

Today, I look back at spending approximately two months every summer in the 1950s in Wisconsin. What a great time to be a kid and grow up. What a wonderful life!

James Halstead Smith was born and raised in Nashville, Tennessee. He attended John Overton High School in Nashville and graduated from Western Kentucky University, Bowling Green, Kentucky.

He retired from the U.S. Army (active duty and Army Reserves) as a Lieutenant Colonel. Jim enjoyed a 35-year career at Third National Bank (which merged into SunTrust Bank) in Nashville. His third career position (10 ½ years) was as the Assistant City Administrator and Finance Director for the City of Spring Hill, Tennessee.

Jim has written two previous books, both published in 2023. Robertson Academy School, A History, a (now public) grammar school in Nashville that began in 1806 via legislation from the State of Tennessee. His second book, Priest - Smith, A Family History, is a book about four individuals in his family, his Smith grandparents and that grandmother's parents, Eugene and Bettie Priest.

The Peninsula, Ramsthal's Nagawicka Lake Subdivision, is about his maternal grandmother's family who developed the Ramsthal's Nagawicka Lake Subdivision.